Graphic Organizers in Science™

Learning About Heat and Temperature with Graphic Organizers

Julie Fiedler

The Rosen Publishing Group's
PowerKids Press™
New York

For my family, with love and appreciation

Published in 2007 by The Rosen Publishing Group, Inc.
29 East 21st Street, New York, NY 10010

First Edition

Editor: Jennifer Way
Layout Design: Julio A. Gil

Photo Credits: Cover (center), p. 8 © Todd Pearson/Getty Images; cover (top left), p. 12 (top left) © Digital Vision/Elements of Nature; cover (top right), p. 12 (bottom right) © www.istockphoto.com/Elena Elisseeva; cover (bottom left), pp. 11 (center), 12 (bottom, second from left) © www.istockphoto.com/Diane Diederich; cover (bottom right), p. 12 (top right) © www.istockphoto.com/Popi Dimakou; p. 7 (top) Map Resources; p. 7 (center) © Timothy Shonnard/Getty Images; p. 7 (bottom) © Jim Sugar/Corbis; p. 11 (left) © www.istockphoto.com/AbackPhotography; p. 11 (right) © www.istockphoto.com/Mika Makkonen; p. 12 (top center) © www.istockphoto.com/ngirish; p. 12 (bottom, third from left) © www.istockphoto.com/Oleg Prikhodko; p. 12 (bottom left) © www.istockphoto.com/Sharon Meredith; p. 15 (left) © Grace/zefa/Corbis; p. 15 (center) © www.istockphoto.com/Eddy Lund; p. 15 (right) © www.istockphoto.com/Robert Kyllo; p. 16 © Royalty-Free/Corbis; p. 19 © Roy Morsch/Corbis.

Library of Congress Cataloging-in-Publication Data

Fiedler, Julie.
  Learning about heat and temperature with graphic organizers / Julie Fiedler.— 1st ed.
      p. cm. — (Graphic organizers in science)
  Includes index.
  ISBN 1-4042-3408-X (library binding)
  1. Heat—Juvenile literature. 2. Temperature—Juvenile literature. I. Title. II. Series.
  QC256.F54 2007
  536—dc22
                                    2005025628

Manufactured in the United States of America

Contents

Heat and Temperature   5

How Temperature Is Measured   6

Weather and Temperature   9

The Effects of Heat   10

What Causes Changes in Heat and Temperature?   13

Heat Transfer   14

Conduction   17

Convection   18

Radiation   21

Everyday Energy   22

Glossary   23

Index   24

Web Sites   24

KWL Chart: Heat and Temperature

What I **K**now	What I **W**ant to Know	What I've **L**earned
• I can feel the difference between something that is hot and something that is cold.	• How do I know how hot or cold something is?	• By using a thermometer, you will get a temperature reading. Temperature is a number that tells you how hot or cold something is.
• Water freezes and melts.	• How does water change back and forth?	• Heat changes the speed at which molecules vibrate, or move quickly. As the molecules speed up or slow down, water will melt or freeze. This change in the water is known as a change in state.
• I must drink lots of water in the summer.	• What is heat stroke?	• As people get hot, their bodies lose water in the form of sweat to cool down. If people do not drink enough water, they will get a sickness known as heat stroke.
• Sand gets hotter faster than water does.	• Why do different things heat at different speeds?	• Everything takes in and gives off heat at different rates. Water takes longer to take in heat than does sand, so sand will heat up faster than water.

Heat and Temperature

Everything in the world is made up of millions of tiny parts called atoms. Atoms group together to make **molecules**. Each molecule vibrates, or moves quickly. **Energy** causes this vibration. Everything in the world has energy, from a running animal to a burning stove to an ice cube.

One type of energy is called heat energy. The faster the molecules move, the more heat they have. Scientists measure how hot things are by using **temperature**. Temperature is a number stated in **degrees**. Things that are hot, such as fire, have a lot of heat and a high temperature. Things that are cold, such as ice cubes, do not have much heat and therefore have a low temperature. Temperature is measured using a **thermometer**.

KWL organizers help you realize what you know about a subject, what questions you have about it, and what you can learn about it through study. You can make your own KWL chart and fill in the third column as you learn.

How Temperature Is Measured

Temperature measurements can be given on three different scales. These are Kelvin, Celsius, and Fahrenheit. Scientists use Kelvin. Celsius is used in countries that use the **metric system**, such as Canada. The United States uses the Fahrenheit scale. Each scale has a different number reading for the same temperature. For example, water freezes at 32° Fahrenheit, which is the same as 0° Celsius.

The most common type of thermometer is a liquid thermometer. Liquid **mercury** is placed inside a glass tube. The tube has markings on it. When the mercury gets hot, it expands, or grows larger. Then it rises in the tube. When the mercury gets cool, it gets lower in the tube. The tube's numbered markings tell what the temperature is when the mercury is at that mark.

A line graph shows how things change. This line graph shows the change in temperature in California throughout a day in January and a day in June. Find the hour along the bottom and the temperature on the left. California has a mild climate and does not get either very hot in summer or very cold in winter.

Line Graph: Temperature Changes

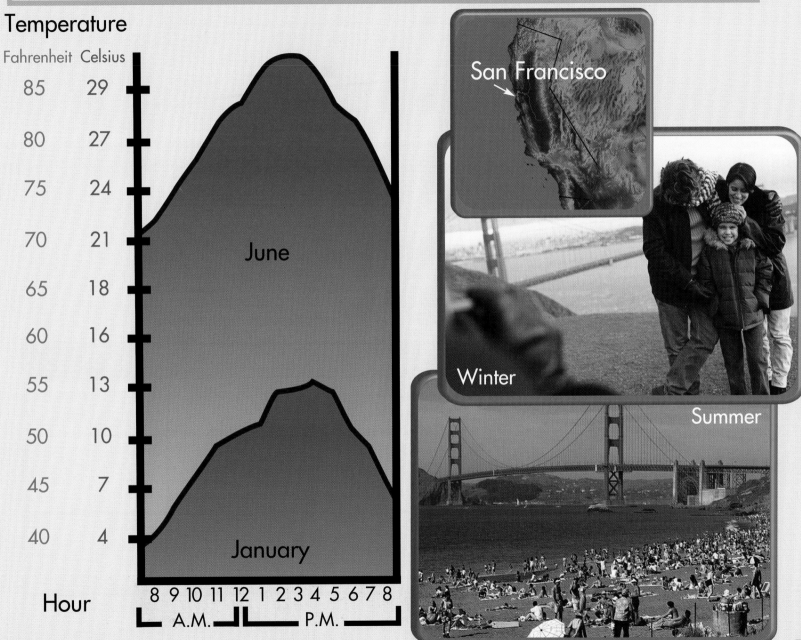

Temperature

Fahrenheit | Celsius
85 | 29
80 | 27
75 | 24
70 | 21
65 | 18
60 | 16
55 | 13
50 | 10
45 | 7
40 | 4

June

January

San Francisco

Winter

Summer

Hour

8 9 10 11 12 1 2 3 4 5 6 7 8

A.M. P.M.

Compare/Contrast Chart: Seasons

Season	Winter	Spring	Summer	Fall
Day/night length	Short days, long nights	Days get longer, nights get shorter	Long days, short nights	Days get shorter, nights get longer
General temperature	At its lowest, the coldest time of year	Begins to rise	At its highest, the the hottest time of year	Begin to fall
Months of the season in North America	December–February	March–May	June–August	September–November
How people deal with it	Wear warm clothes, use heaters	Wear lighter clothes, use fans	Wear lighter clothes, use air conditioners and fans	Wear warmer clothes

Weather and Temperature

The Sun supplies Earth with light and heat and has an effect on its temperature and weather. If you put one thermometer in the shade and one in the sunlight, they will show that the temperature is lower in the shade. As Earth spins different areas are **exposed** to the Sun. This spinning causes day and night. As Earth turns around the Sun, the seasons change. From June to September, North America **tilts** closer to the Sun and has long days and warm summers. From December to March, North America tilts away from the Sun and has shorter days and cold winters.

Different parts of the world have different **climates** because they are exposed to different amounts of sunlight. For example, Antarctica at the South Pole is covered in ice year-round. The Caribbean Islands near the **equator** are warm year-round.

Compare/contrast charts show what two or more things have in common and what differences they have. This chart shows the differences among the seasons in North America.

The Effects of Heat

Heat can change the state of things. When enough heat is applied to water, it boils. Then it turns from a liquid into a gas called water vapor, or steam. Water boils at 212° F (100° C). This temperature is water's boiling point.

Water can also turn from a liquid to a solid. When its temperature is lowered to 32° F (0° C), water turns to ice. This is water's freezing point. Different things have different freezing, melting, and boiling points. Water melts at 32° F (0° C). Steel melts at 2,500° F (1,371° C)!

Heat can change objects without changing their states. For example, if metal gets hot, it expands. The Eiffel Tower in Paris, France, can become more than 1 inch (2.5 cm) taller on a hot day!

This chart shows how facts can be organized. This chart tells how changes in temperature have an effect on the states of water.

Chart: States of Water

Boiling Point (212° F, 100° C)

Freezing Point (32° F, 0° C)

Melting Point (32° F, 0° C)

State	Temperature Point	What Happens	Example
Liquid	Boiling Point (212° F, 100° C)	Liquid becomes gas	Water turns to steam
Liquid	Freezing Point (32° F, 0° C)	Liquid becomes solid	Water turns to ice
Solid	Melting Point (32° F, 0° C)	Solid becomes liquid	Ice turns to water
Gas	Deposition Point	Gas becomes solid	Water vapor turns to frost

Concept Web: Things That Cause Changes in Temperature

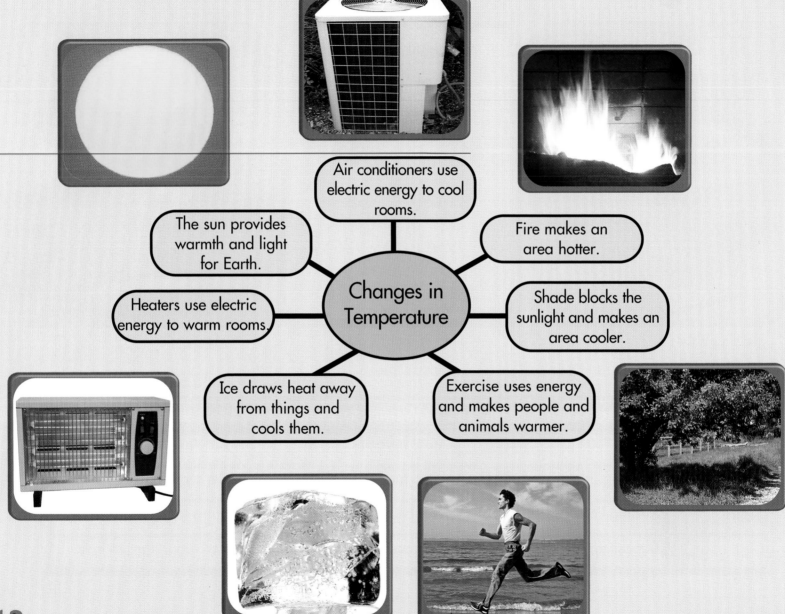

Air conditioners use electric energy to cool rooms.

Fire makes an area hotter.

The sun provides warmth and light for Earth.

Heaters use electric energy to warm rooms.

Changes in Temperature

Shade blocks the sunlight and makes an area cooler.

Ice draws heat away from things and cools them.

Exercise uses energy and makes people and animals warmer.

What Causes Changes in Heat and Temperature?

Many things can cause changes in heat and temperature. There are two main ways that these changes happen. First, heat changes when energy is used. For example, people produce heat all the time. That is because the body's operations, such as heartbeats, use energy and give off heat. A person's usual temperature is 98.6° F (37° C). As people use energy to exercise, they produce more heat and will have a higher temperature.

Heat also changes when two or more things interact with one another. Heat passes from one thing to another, which is called heat transfer. For example, the Sun is a natural **source** of heat that warms Earth. Fire is another source of heat that increases the temperature of things around it. Cooking is another good example. A stove heats a pot, which then heats food.

A concept web is a graphic organizer with a main idea in the middle. Facts and examples are added around the subject. You can add more facts as you learn about the subject. This concept web shows different things that have an effect on heat and temperature.

Heat Transfer

Heat is always moving from one thing to another to create balance. Heat moves from an area with a higher temperature, called a heat source. Heat moves to an area with a lower temperature, called a heat sink. This is called heat transfer.

The heat from a stove raising the temperature of a pot of water is an example of heat transfer at work. If you have an air-conditioned room and you fill it with people, the room will become warmer because everyone's body heat raises the temperature. This is also an example of heat transfer. There are three ways that heat transfers from heat source to heat sink. These are called **conduction**, **convection**, and **radiation**.

A tree chart shows the subject of the graphic organizer in the trunk. Elements of the subject are added as branches. This chart shows the different types of heat transfer.

Tree Chart: Heat Transfer

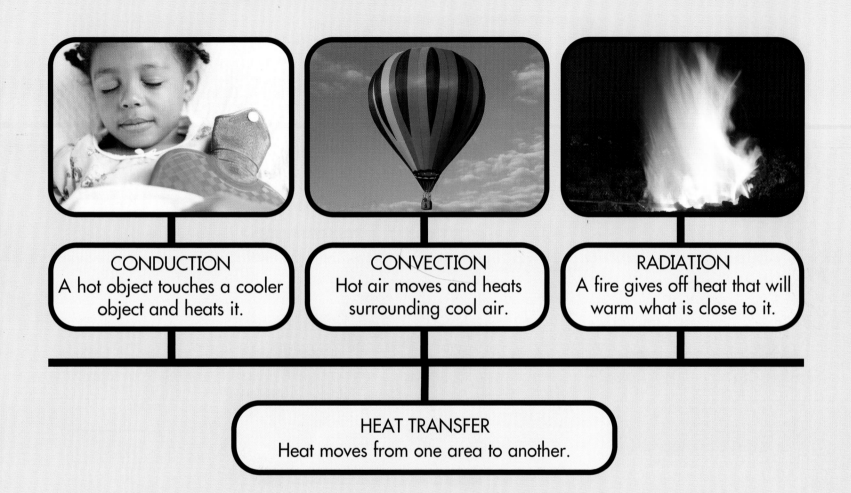

CONDUCTION
A hot object touches a cooler object and heats it.

CONVECTION
Hot air moves and heats surrounding cool air.

RADIATION
A fire gives off heat that will warm what is close to it.

HEAT TRANSFER
Heat moves from one area to another.

Sequence Chart: Conduction

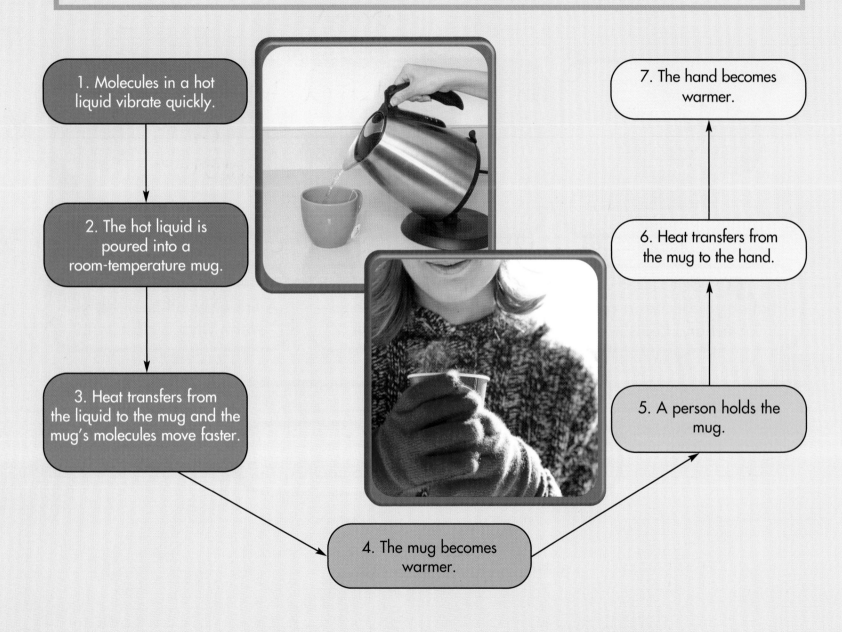

1. Molecules in a hot liquid vibrate quickly.

2. The hot liquid is poured into a room-temperature mug.

3. Heat transfers from the liquid to the mug and the mug's molecules move faster.

4. The mug becomes warmer.

5. A person holds the mug.

6. Heat transfers from the mug to the hand.

7. The hand becomes warmer.

Conduction

One form of heat transfer is called conduction. Conduction occurs when two solid objects of different temperature touch each other. Heat passes from the heat source to the heat sink at the point where the two objects touch. If you touch the sidewalk on a hot summer day, heat from the sidewalk will spread to your hand. Your hand will become warm.

Some things conduct heat better than others do because of the way their atoms are arranged. Metal is a good conductor because it transfers heat quickly and well. Wood is not a good conductor because it does not transfer heat well. Sometimes having a poor conductor is a good thing. If you were cooking, you would want a metal pan to heat the food. You would stir with a wooden spoon so you would not burn your hand.

A sequence chart shows the order of steps that happen in a process. This sequence chart shows how conduction works.

Convection

Convection is the heat transfer of liquids and gases. Hot liquids and gases rise, making room for cooler liquid or gas below. As the hot and cold parts of the liquids or gases move, heat is transferred across the areas.

An example of convection is boiling water. As a pot heats, the water touching it heats through conduction and rises. Cooler water sinks, gets heated, and then rises. As this **process** continues, all the water will be heated and will boil. Because this movement happens naturally, it is called free convection.

Forced convection uses an outside means to move the liquid or gas. For example, a heater with a fan forces the hot air to move over a greater area. This forces movement of the hot air and the cold air so the heater can warm a larger area.

This graphic organizer is a cycle chart. A cycle chart shows something step-by-step. This cycle chart shows the process of convection when water boils.

Cycle: Boiling Water

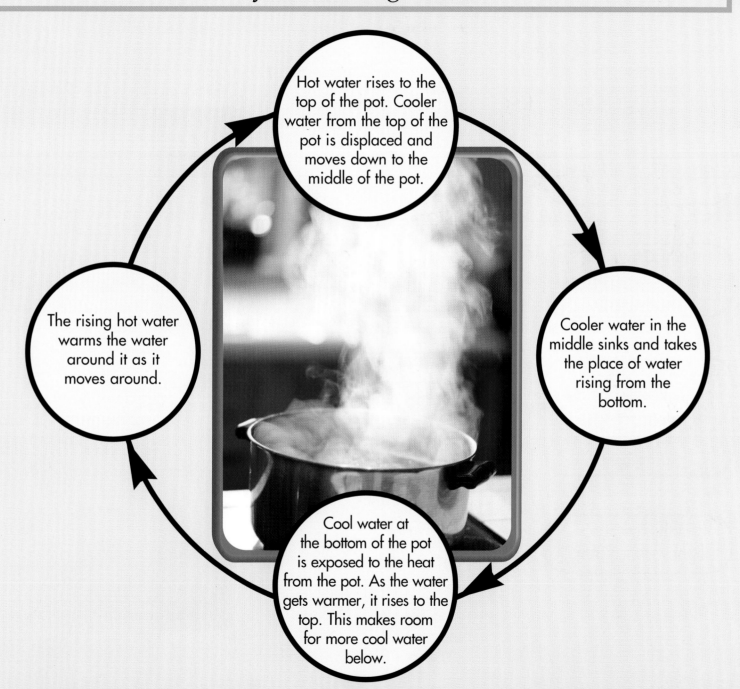

Hot water rises to the top of the pot. Cooler water from the top of the pot is displaced and moves down to the middle of the pot.

Cooler water in the middle sinks and takes the place of water rising from the bottom.

Cool water at the bottom of the pot is exposed to the heat from the pot. As the water gets warmer, it rises to the top. This makes room for more cool water below.

The rising hot water warms the water around it as it moves around.

19

Flow Chart: The Sun's Radiation

Sun: Radiates, or gives off, heat in the form of light.

↓

Light: Travels in waves. These waves are energy.

↓

Colors: Not all light is visible, or able to be seen. Visible light is one part of the Sun's light.

↓

Earth: The Sun's light warms Earth.

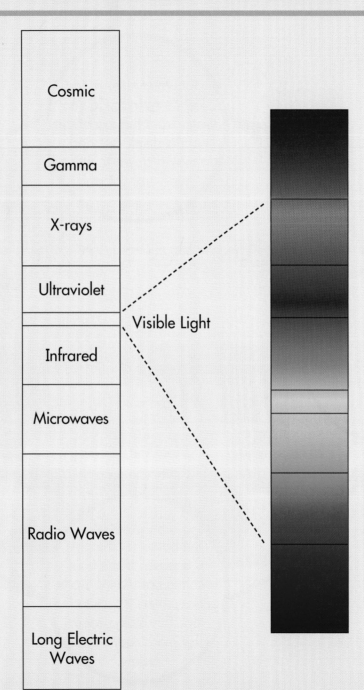

Cosmic

Gamma

X-rays

Ultraviolet

Visible Light

Infrared

Microwaves

Radio Waves

Long Electric Waves

Radiation

The last type of heat transfer is called radiation. In conduction and convection, heat is transferred directly from one object to another. In radiation heat can be given off in a vacuum. This is a scientific term meaning the lack of any solid, liquid, or even gas. Radiation works as **particles**, which make up molecules and atoms, give off **infrared** waves. This is a type of **electromagnetic** energy. These infrared waves cause the particles to vibrate, or move quickly. As the particles vibrate, they give off heat.

The Sun radiates heat through space, which is a vacuum, to warm Earth. People also give off radiant heat, which can be picked up. For example, burglar alarms and night-vision glasses pick up infrared waves.

This graphic organizer is called a flow chart. This flow chart explains how the sun's radiation travels from outer space to Earth. The picture on the right shows the different types of waves the Sun gives off. This is called the electromagnetic spectrum. Visible light is the smallest part of the spectrum.

Everyday Energy

The seasons can be either naturally hot or cold, and machines such as air conditioners and heaters can be used to make different temperatures more comfortable. These machines use a lot of **electricity** to make homes cooler or warmer. Electric companies use **natural resources** to make electricity, and it costs money to use electricity.

Now that you know more about heat transfer, you can think of other ways to change heat and temperature using less energy. For example, the Sun radiates heat and Earth gets hot in summer. Shade provided by trees or blinds will help block the sunlight and keep the shady area cooler. Fans use less electricity than air conditioners do. Fans are an example of how forced convection can be used to help keep climates more comfortable. By using these things, you can help **conserve** energy.

Glossary

climates (KLY-mits) The kind of weather a certain area has.

conduction (kun-DUK-shun) The direct passing of heat from a warmer object to a cooler one.

conserve (kun-SERV) To keep something from being wasted or used up.

convection (kun-VEK-shun) The type of heat transfer in which liquids and gases are heated.

degrees (dih-GREEZ) A measurement of temperature.

electricity (ih-lek-TRIH-suh-tee) Energy that produces light, heat, or motion.

electromagnetic (ih-lek-troh-mag-NEH-tik) Having a force of magnetism created by a small bit of electricity.

energy (EH-nur-jee) The power to work or to act.

equator (ih-KWAY-tur) An imaginary line around Earth that separates it into two parts, northern and southern.

exposed (ik-SPOHZD) Left open.

infrared (in-fruh-RED) Light waves that are outside of the visible part of the light range at the red end, which we can see.

mercury (MER-kyuh-ree) A poisonous, silver-colored element.

metric system (MEH-trik SIS-tem) A method of measurement based on counting tens.

molecules (MAH-lih-kyoolz) Two or more atoms joined together.

natural resources (NA-chuh-rul REE-sors-ez) Things in nature that can be used by people.

particles (PAR-tih-kulz) Small pieces of something.

process (PRAH-ses) A set of actions done in a certain order.

radiation (ray-dee-AY-shun) Rays of light, heat, or energy that spread outward from something.

source (SORS) The place from which something starts.

temperature (TEM-pur-cher) How hot or cold something is.

thermometer (ther-MAH-meh-ter) An instrument used to measure temperature.

tilts (TILTS) Raises or tips into a sloped or angled position.

Index

A

atoms, 5, 17

B

boiling point, 10

C

Celsius scale, 6
climates, 9, 22
conduction, 14, 17, 21
conductor, 17
convection, 14, 18, 21

E

electricity, 22

electromagnetic energy, 21

F

Fahrenheit scale, 6
freezing point, 10

H

heat sink, 14, 17
heat source, 14, 17
heat transfer, 13–14, 17, 21

I

infrared waves, 21

K

Kelvin scale, 6

L

liquid thermometer, 6

M

melting point, 10
molecules, 5, 21

R

radiation, 14, 21

T

thermometer, 5, 9

Web Sites

Due to the changing nature of Internet links, PowerKids Press has developed an online list of Web sites related to the subject of this book. This site is updated regularly. Please use this link to access the list: www.powerkidslinks.com/gosci/heat/